# DEEP STATE

# DEEP STATE

The truth about the secret
US "Shadow Government" ruling America
and how you can fight and beat it
before they take everything from you

DEAN MILLER

Printed in the United States of America

First Printing, 2017

ISBN 978-0-9974376-7-6

5280 Publishing, LLC dba AmericanSurvivor.com
453 E. Wonderview Ave.
Estes Park, CO 80517
www.AmericanSurvivor.com

## DISCLAIMER OF LIABILITY AND WARRANTY

## COPYRIGHT



## TERMS AND DISCLAIMER

By using, viewing, and interacting with this guide or the AmericanSurvivor.com.com website, you agree to all terms of engagement, thus assuming complete responsibility for your own actions.

The authors and publishers will not be held liable or claim accountability for any loss or injuries. Use, view, and interact with these resources at your own risk. All publications from AmericanSurvivor.com and its related companies are strictly for informational purposes only.

While all attempts have been made to verify the accuracy of information provided on our website and within our publications, neither the authors nor the publishers are responsible for assuming liability for possible inaccuracies. The authors and publishers disclaim any responsibility for the inaccuracy of the content, including but not limited to errors or omissions. Loss of property, injury to self or others, and even death could occur as a direct or indirect consequence of the use and application of any content found herein.

Did you vote in the past election? Have you ever voted? Did you think that your vote could make a difference, somehow swaying the tide of a nationwide election so that your chosen candidate could win? We hate to start an information guide with a question, much less three of them in a row, but what we are about to tell you is so startling that you will question everything you think you know about American politics.

Let's start with a quick lesson on middle school civics. You know that every four years, America comes together to vote for and select its next president. Similarly, every two years congressmen are elected, and every six years, we select our senators. These three groups comprise the dual institutions of the Executive branch as well as Congress. We are oversimplifying this somewhat, as there are many other elections running constantly in America, from gubernatorial elections all the way down to city elections. Generally speaking, the person with the most votes stands the best chance of winning, and we are taught early on as children that if we seek to effect change, we must vote such that we

YOUR VOTE COUNTS

can pick who we want in office. It's an elegant system on paper; if we are unhappy with the current mayor, assemblyman, councilman, governor, senator, congressman, or even president, all we need to do is cast our vote to let our voice be heard.

*Except for it's a lie.* The entire "democratic" system that exists within the United States today is a sham, a mere sideshow that most Americans believe actually means something. Your vote is meaningless for one important reason: the person you vote for is powerless to do anything meaningful, utterly incapable of effecting any significant change. It doesn't matter whether you vote Republican or Democrat; *your candidate will not be able to change a thing.* Please don't confuse what we are saying; we are not repeating the oft parroted comment that deep down, Republicans and Democrats share the same ideology. That's preposterous, and we know full well that they share almost opposite opinions on most topics that affect the American people. What we are saying is that either a Republican or Democrat viewpoint is utterly irrelevant because the person who is elected will not be able to change anything significantly either way, *because the Deep State won't let them.*

If you have never heard of the term *Deep State* (sometimes referred to as Shadow Government), we'll forgive you for not knowing. You won't find the Deep State on the evening news or in the paper. You won't see a Yahoo headline telling you what the Deep State is up to. You won't see a commercial on TV trumpeting the Deep State's latest moves. They are a mystery to most people, but be warned, the Deep State holds all the power and makes *all* the decisions — the ones that count anyways.

Before we tell you just what the Deep State is exactly, we're going to continue our civics lesson. The American constitution and system of government is beautiful in its simplicity, an elegant system designed by righteous men who truly believed what they wrote and tried their best to guard against corruption. Rest assured, the Founding Fathers did a good job setting up government — in fact, they did such a good job that the constitution is still the only thing hindering the Deep State from fulfilling its evil designs. So if the Founding Fathers had it right, and the constitution is right, then where did all this go wrong?

In a word, what went wrong was the sheer size of government; the Founders never imagined that the government would ever get to be so massive; the government was supposed to be a minimalist apparatus that served the people. While they were alive, it more or less did just that, but soon after their deaths, the government began to grow. Like a cancer, it kept silently expanding to the point where a hundred years after the Founders died, it was massive, and two hundred years later, it was a gargantuan monster that was never, ever envisioned by the Founders in their wildest nightmares. Today, it is even bigger, wields powers that were never dreamt of

by the Founders, and is more or less unstoppable regardless of who currently lives in the White House.

This government is now a mutant tumor that is threatening to destroy America, and deep within this tumor is the Deep State, what could be called the core of the disease. Like a cancer, the Deep State has no leader, no governor, no spokesperson. The Deep State may not even know who all belongs to it, and Deep State operatives may not report to anyone. Like cancerous cells, Deep State operatives are fully functioning nodes capable of reproducing their ideology to new converts; they are decentralized and almost undetectable, but they are there. Keep in mind that some people link the Deep State with Freemasonry, Illuminati, extra-terrestrials, and the Bilderberg group but the true Deep State has nothing at all to do with X-Files style content, and the tin foil hat crowd is just a distraction from what is really going on. In fact, the spectacular link of the Deep State to popular yet laughable conspiracy theories is one of the covers used by this evil apparatus.

Still don't believe that something evil exists? Check out the quote below:

> *"Today the path to total dictatorship in the U.S. can be laid by strictly legal means, unseen and unheard by Congress, the President, or the people. Outwardly we have a Constitutional government. We have operating within our government and political system ... a well-organized political-action group*

*in this country, determined to destroy our Constitution and establish a one-party state.... The important point to remember about this group is not its ideology but its organization... It operates secretly, silently, continuously to transform our Government.... This group ... is answerable neither to the President, the Congress, nor the courts. It is practically irremovable."*

— Senator William Jenner, 1954 speech

That quote was written in *1954 — 63 years ago*. Elements of the Deep State were in place over half century ago. Today, it's much worse.

# COG, COUSIN OF DEEP STATE

COG, or Continuity Of Government, is a decent idea on its surface. Beyond the normal lines of presidential succession, there exists a secondary government that is there just in case the primary line of government is wiped out. Sounds like a nice safety blanket, and a prudent measure, but it's mostly a leftover relic from the days of nuclear threats from Soviets. In effect, the personnel that comprise COG are wholly unelected officials that nobody knows about who wield immense powers that no one really controls, and they are right there, poised to rule over us should the primary government be wiped out in a nuclear strike, taken away by aliens, or consumed by a zombie apocalypse. It's kind of funny that those three events, however remote, are the only things that could really cause the thousands of people who comprise the primary government to disappear, yet we have a backup plan in the event they do.

COG is more than just a backup plan in reality, and a government that clings to power desperately even creates contingency plans in the event of its own demise. The shadowy people who comprise COG are unknown to the masses, yet working in government *right now* in parallel with their elected counterparts, ready to assume control whenever needed. You didn't vote for anyone in COG, you don't know any of them, you've never read their tabloid news, and you didn't watch their campaign commercials. They are next in line to run the country, and guess what — their identities are *classified*.

# DEEP STATE MUSCLE

Before we tell you more about who the Deep State is, let's focus for a minute on Deep State's bite, which is a lot worse than its bark. First and foremost, realize that without muscle, the Deep State would be powerless and would be easily overthrown. Secondly, realize that the military of the United States is one of the Deep State's worst enemies, so it's decided to do a little preparing of its own in the past hundred years. Allow us to explain.

The United States military is comprised of the Army, Navy, Air Force, Marine Corps and Coast Guard. There are strict federal controls on everything having to do with the military; as an example:

- There can be, by law, only so many soldiers.
- There can be, by law, only so many Generals, so many Admirals.

- There is a mandatory retirement age in all branches of the military.
- There are strict controls on what the military can do, and also what it cannot do.
- Only certain *elected officials* can directly control the military.

The Founding Fathers were scared to death of the military, and for good reason. In their day and age, the British military was used as heavy handed police here in the American colonies. They kicked people out of their own homes and stole them for their own lodgings. The Founding Fathers therefore decided to legally hamstring the military by placing it under civilian control to avoid a military dictatorship, and they also strictly controlled the size of it during peacetime so that it wouldn't be a menace to the people.

Deep State knows all of this, and knows that the use of the military on domestic soil is strictly prohibited. They also know the military can be a massive threat to the way they do business, so they went and *created their own military*, one that no one knows about. Deep State now has vast armies of militarized police under its control.

These government agency operatives are actually larger in number than the United States Military, and possess the following equipment:

- Helicopters and airplanes
- Drones
- Fully automatic weapons
- Heavily armored blast resistant armored vehicles, and in some cases, tanks
- Full body armor
- Explosives
- Federal powers of arrest and apprehension

If the above sounds like the description of an army, it is! And guess what, all of this nationwide Army belongs to a bureaucratic Deep State, who hides these soldiers in plain sight. Some of the Departments it uses to hide these soldiers in are ludicrous:

- Energy Department
- US Forest Service
- Education Department
- Treasury Department

Why any of the above require armored vehicles is beyond us, other than it's a thinly veiled ploy to keep what amounts to a standing army on our soil, exactly what the Founders wanted to avoid. It gets better; the armies of the Deep State:

- Are not controlled by any elected official
- Are bigger in number than the US Military
- Have no limits on how big they can grow to
- Have no limits as to what they can do
- Can operate on American soil and basically do whatever they please

Militarized police and government agencies are a direct creation of the Deep State, one of the more shocking changes that has occurred in the past 20-30 years, and one of the Deep State's latest achievements. You didn't think the Deep State would go out quietly, did you?

# DEEP STATE EYES AND EARS

Even though it has a sizeable army, the Deep State would be blind and deaf if it didn't possess a way to find out what's going on. Not only does the Deep State possess a world class intelligence apparatus, it in fact has the largest information gathering system on the *planet*. Deep State is spying on you 24/7 with its intelligence partners:

- CIA — Central Intelligence Agency
- NSA — National Security Agency
- FBI — Federal Bureau of Investigation
- About two dozen domestic intelligence agencies you'vc never heard of

Whenever it can, Deep State listens in to your phone calls, reads your texts and emails, records your voice, and photographs you both on earth and *from space.* They can know virtually anything about you, and they have billions of dollars annually with which to spy on you. How about manpower? Deep State possesses 854,000 contractors with *top secret clearances.* Note that this is more personnel with top secret clearances than the government actually has! All of these shadowy federal agencies are intertwined with State and local police agencies to create one of the most extreme surveillance states ever conceived, one in which every American is spied upon virtually all of the time.

# PORTRAIT OF A BUREAUCRAT

Let's take a look at a powerful Deep State operative, a literal example of what a Deep Stater looks like. Since we don't know exactly who these people are, we're going to create a fictional person that illustrates the qualities and behaviors of successful Deep Staters. We'll call this person Jim for convenience. Everything within this is fictional, but you get the idea.

After graduating from college with a bachelor's degree, Jim got an internship with the Bureau of Tobacco and Firearms (ATF). Initially, he was going to continue his studies, but the internship turned into a job offer, and Jim decided to stick around. He wasn't the least bit interested in actual law enforcement; Jim's skillset was mainly organizational in nature and he was very good at writing manuals, instructions, and procedures. Jim even had a detailed operating procedure for his coffee machine at home.

Jim originally started out in the Dallas field office of the ATF (that's where he was from), but as he promoted within the organization, he was transferred to half a dozen different field offices, finally landing in Washington DC, where he was the chief architect behind dozens of the ATF's policies and procedures. In fact, the regulations that Jim helped write held the force of law in the United States, even though Jim wasn't an elected lawmaker, and none of his regulations were ever voted on or even commented on by the public. Jim was proud of his accomplishments at the ATF; although never owning a firearm in his life (he did shoot one once, however), Jim created all sorts of regulations pertaining to magazine capacity, barrel length, and caliber size. Being someone who wasn't inherently interested in guns, Jim's personal view was that the average American was a little too interested in guns for his liking.

Occasionally, Jim would have a boss that had different ideas than Jim did about firearms. In fact, one of his bosses reminded Jim about the 2nd Amendment of the United States Constitution, and told Jim that his regulations should reflect the right of the people to keep and bear arms. Jim didn't much like that boss, and soon he was replaced with a boss that thought more like Jim did. Jim climbed higher and higher in within the ATF, and soon enough he had been with the agency for over 25 years, far longer than any president stayed in office.

Sometimes, America would get a pro-gun president, and the ATF would receive directives to loosen up some of Jim's regulations. But Jim knew that this was mostly talk, and that in the event of extreme pressure, Jim could just slow his work down to a crawl and simply wait the president out. After all, there was no term on Jim's service; he could remain at the agency until he was dead, and it was also functionally impossible to fire him because

although he could be inefficient at times, Jim had done nothing grossly negligent enough to be fired.

By the time Jim turned 60, he was the Deputy Director of the ATF. No newspaper reported on his activities; he could walk the streets anonymously and no one knew who he was. Occasionally his boss, the Director of the ATF would be sacked symbolically, and in those times Jim would be the acting director, but he would always be bumped back down when the next appointee was placed; which suited Jim just fine, because having 30+ years on the job made him more knowledgeable and more powerful than anyone else in the agency, *including the Director.* Sure, the Director made some noise now and then, but Jim was calling all of the shots. When he was given a directive he agreed with, he fast tracked it and made it happen. When he was given a directive he didn't agree with, he would stall (sometimes for years), miring the order in red tape to the point that his superiors either gave up or forgot about it.

Jim's career spanned three decades, and he wrote regulations that were just like laws, sending many people to jail. Jim was never elected, never appointed by a president. He just started out as an intern, and stubbornly clung to his job while being promoted. Jim reigned longer than any president or elected official *ever.*

## DO YOU GET IT?

The Deep State is comprised of people just like Jim. They are judges, police chiefs, government agents, bureaucrats, staffers, and political party officials. They obtain their jobs humbly, then stick around for decades putting their spin on everything they touch, clinging to power. They have no sense of service, all they care about is their own spheres of influence. They will bring the will of any elected official to a grinding halt, and despite congress making an elaborate show of passing laws and effecting change, the Deep State can stop congress dead in its tracks. It can kill anything with red tape or simply waiting out the current term of the elected officials. Deep State, therefore, has become more powerful than any elected official, *even all of them combined.*

# FIGHT THE DEEP STATE!

If we have painted a picture of hopelessness, if we have shown you a glimpse of the Deep State which is seemingly all powerful and you are worried, then we have achieved our goal; hopefully we can spur you to action. So how do you fight an enemy with billions of dollars, with an army at its disposal, and with the capability to spy on you 24/7? It won't be easy, but there is a way. In order to fight the Deep State at its own game, you need a multi-pronged approach to succeed. You will also need discipline and commitment, because your new way of life will not be easy, since old habits die hard.

# PERSONAL ANONYMITY – THE SECRET WEAPON AGAINST DEEP STATE

The less Deep State knows about you, the less control they will have over you. Being anonymous in this day and age is hard, but it is worth it. Here are some expert tips on how to do just that.

- **Use a Prepaid wireless phone** (i.e. a Burner Phone). You can buy a prepaid burner phone at places like Wal-Mart and Target for under $20. To add minutes to the phone, you simply buy a prepaid card at the same store. *At no time do you ever have to use your real name to use the phone.* It's a completely anonymous way to make phone calls and send messages without having a government agency know who you are. There are some caveats, however. First of all, your phone can still be wiretapped, although it will be far more difficult for someone to determine who owns the phone because there is no name associated with the account.

Secondly, whoever you are calling could also be wiretapped, so watch what you say and text. Just using a burner phone alone is an excellent way to stymie the Deep State.

- **Avoid popular so-called free service providers like the plague.** Have you ever wondered why something that is so useful to you is offered free? Have you ever stopped to think how Google, Gmail, Hotmail, Facebook, Twitter, or Instagram are able to provide gigabyte after gigabyte of free services to you for *years* and yet not charge you a dime? Guess what — they are selling your information, and not all of it is being sold to friendly advertising companies like you think it is. The Deep State is an information maniac, and is actively colluding with government agencies like the NSA and CIA to scan your data and learn everything about you. Avoid free internet services; they are not as free as you think.

- **Use encryption religiously.** The Deep State has access to the world's best supercomputers, but it would still take those supercomputers decades to break even a simple encryption algorithm. You should be actively encrypting your email communications as well as your entire hard drive. It's easier than you think to do this, and it is very effective against all kinds of intrusive attacks, even if they manage to take your entire computer away.

- **Purchase a mail box and use it for everything.** Although you are required to show ID and provide an address to pick up a mailbox at somewhere like Mail Boxes Etc. or the UPS Store, your proof of identity resides within the store, and the store owner simply has to keep it on hand. Those forms aren't sent anywhere, and although the Deep State can easily obtain them, it won't unless you raise suspicion. In the meantime, you get the benefit of routing all of your mail and using the mail box store as your legal address, which throws off the nosy bloodhounds who like to track these sorts of things. Don't get a Post Office PO box — instead go for one at a mail box store that looks like a street address.

# BEWARE THE SURVEILLANCE STATE

You are being watched all the time. The sooner you realize this, the better off you will be, and the Deep State's agency of choice for spying is the Central Intelligence Agency — the mighty CIA. Here are seven tips to avoid this and thwart the Deep State:

## Rule #1: Assume every word you utter is being recorded.

Between cell phones that act as bugs to TVs with fake off modes, you are likely being eavesdropped upon and don't even know it. Be very careful of what you say with electronic devices of any kind present in the room. Consider that many homes have small rooms where no electronic devices are present (closets, mud rooms, bathrooms). Consider using these rooms to speak sensitive things in a very, very low whisper to your spouse, relative, or child. Direct communications like this in closed rooms where no eavesdropping equipment is present are *extremely* hard to listen in on, even with the Deep State's powerful tools.

## Rule#2: No internet = no data relay

The simple act of recording audio, video, or pictures of you is useless without the ability to transmit this data back to the CIA. The CIA uses two methods of data transmission; cell phone wireless networks for your phone, and wired or Wi-Fi internet. Absent these two transmission methods, there is no way for this stolen data to make its way back to people who can use it. Really paranoid? *Unplug your Wi-Fi router or hub at night or whenever it's not in use.* It might be inconvenient to start it up whenever you want to use the internet (kind of like an old dial up connection), but at least data will not be transmitted without your knowledge. Also, be mindful of neighbors with Wi-Fi enabled; even if you shut your router down, the CIA can still use other Wi-Fi connections that are present...

## Rule #3: Electronic devices need power to run

Sounds obvious, but an easy way to defeat a CIA hack like "fake off mode" on a TV is to simply unplug the device when it's not in use. Fake off works because the TV still has power to it by being plugged into the wall, but even the mighty CIA has not figured out how to remotely and wirelessly power devices. Worried that a device might be eavesdropping on you? Unplug it! It cannot work without power and will be unable to transmit, record, or function unless it's plugged into a wall.

## Rule #4: Radio communications can be jammed

Many cell phones lack removable batteries anymore. Once upon a time, if you wanted to make sure your phone was shut off, you would just pull its battery pack (see Rule 3 above), ensuring it was dead. With a built in battery pack that isn't user removable, that's no longer an option, and if the CIA can perfect Fake Off modes with TVs, it can do the same with cell phones. So forget about trying to make sure your phone is off; take a detour and kill the phone's cell signal by putting the cell phone inside of an RF proof plastic bag. These bags are designed to keep sensitive electronics safe from static discharge, but they also have the unintended side effect of jamming the cell signal. In a pinch, you can also wrap the phone in tin foil, which does the exact same thing. With its cell signal jammed, the phone will not be able to transmit or reach the cellular network, which also means it will be useless as an eavesdropping device if it cannot transmit data back to the CIA (see Rule 2)

## Rule #5: Be careful about what you commit to paper

Many terror plots are revealed before, during, or after the action because of the detailed notes that the terrorist kept; things like plans, blueprints, photos, post-it notes, hand writing on memo pads, text messages and emails all are capable of being incriminating evidence. We're not saying you are planning a terror plot, but what we are saying is that the less you write down (physically or electronically), the less the CIA will be able to use against you. The Deep State cannot (as of yet) read minds, and therefore the most truly important information needs to be committed to ***memory***, and if necessary, shared with trusted individuals ***verbally***, in a secure location free from the threat of any eavesdropping. Memories, thoughts, and near silent verbal communication are still un-hackable by the CIA!

## Rule #6: Embrace technology, but don't trust it

While new cars are exciting, fresh, and offer tons of safety features and automation, consider that perhaps you just don't need to live like the Jetsons. Sure, a new car is nice, but a 10 year old car can be just as nice and would be totally free from the threat of remote CIA control and eavesdropping. Many of the technologies that the CIA uses to piggyback its nefarious malware on to just didn't exist even just a few years ago. Consider your safety when choosing that newer vehicle, keeping in mind that just because it has more advanced safety features than an older vehicle, doesn't mean it's necessarily ***safer*** for you.

## Rule #7: Cell phone; friend or foe?

The cell phone is the CIA's dream device; they could not have foreseen how pervasive its use would have been in today's society. It can track your location, listen in to your calls, and read your texts and emails. It can transmit your full browsing history to anyone with a few keystrokes; it can reveal the extent of your research

or ordinary life by sending your pictures to total strangers. Kids have cell phones. Grandpa in the senior's home has a cell phone. Everyone in between has a cell phone. By proximity, even if someone can't hack your phone, the phone on the table of the guy next to you can be hacked and listen in just as effectively. Cell phones are quite literally the perfect surveillance device, and at the same time, a necessity in today's society. Here's what you can do to minimize the effects of your cell:

- Don't necessarily take it with you everywhere you go. It generates a trail of where it's been, so if you need to go somewhere sensitive (cache location for example), *leave it at home.*
- Be careful what you say, write, text, browse, or photograph with the phone. Assume it's all being monitored.
- When not needed, power it down and put it in an RF proof bag.
- Run as few apps and programs on the phone as possible. Any app could be a potential vehicle for CIA malware. Go lean!

# ARM UP

The Deep State likes to track firearms purchases because an armed American is represents a threat to the Deep State's very existence. What if we told you that you could legally make your own guns at home?

You can in fact make your own firearms from the ground up — as many as you want — and never have to deal with ATF form 4473s, dealers, paperwork, or even serial numbers. Anyone can actually make any firearm they want, providing that:

1. The person is not otherwise prohibited from owning a firearm
2. The firearm is not intended for sale (although it can be sold at a later date)
3. The person is not making a machine gun, short barreled shotgun, or any other NFA weapon.

As a matter of fact, the firearms you can make on your own *don't even need to have serial numbers* or markings of any kind. The applicable laws regarding making your own firearm are 18 U.S.C. 922(o) and (r), 26 U.S.C.5822, 27 CFR 478.39, 479.62 and 479.105. Search the United States Code for yourself at http://uscode.house.gov/

You can make your own gun 100% from scratch if you like, and if you possess the necessary expertise to do so. Plans of all kinds exist on the internet — many of them, however, are for machine-guns and prohibited weapons, but hey — plans are plans. They are just drawings. Unless you actually build a prohibited firearm, it's impossible for you to run afoul of the law just by possessing schematics, jigs, or drawings.

Still, making your own functional firearm from plans is an onerous procedure, requiring quite a bit in the way of milling equipment, lathes, precision machinery, and most of all, know how. Sure, the British manufactured Sten Guns and other crude submachine guns during World War II, but we're guessing that some crude, inaccurate weapon is not really what you're after.

Wait — you don't need to make the whole gun — barrel, trigger, countless springs, pistol grip, etc — *you just have to make the receiver.* If you could make only the receiver of an AR, AK, or FAL type weapon, you could just *buy* all of the other non controlled parts! But doesn't it still take lots of work to make a receiver? Aren't there special tools and machining involved? Sure, if you were going to build a receiver from scratch — but there is something much better than that...

# THE 80% RECEIVER OR FRAME

Recall that the receiver is the part of the firearm that is the serialized component and accepts the barrel as well as the fire control group. Still, that receiver, somewhere, starts out as a hunk of metal. A factory worker cuts a block of metal that is intended to be a receiver — is it still a firearm at that stage? Not until it is capable of receiving the fire control group and being functional as a firearm! So if you take that same cube of metal, and drill a single hole in it, is it a firearm? No! Okay, so how about if we take our raw cube of metal, and mill it down to the exact size of the receiver, and drill some holes in it — but not all the holes. Is it a firearm? No!

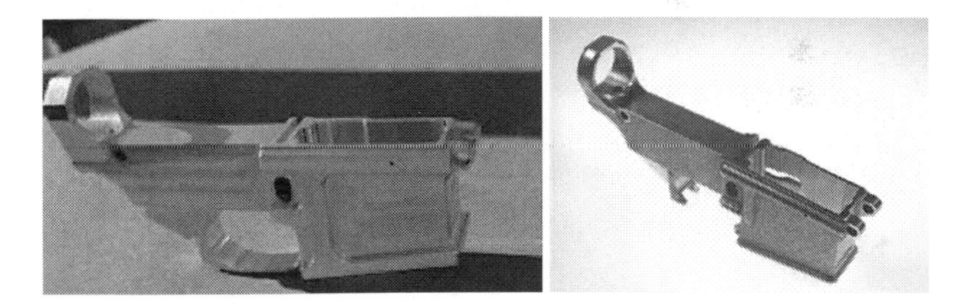

Take a close look at the above pictures — at first glance, they look like a lower receiver, but you know what the ATF calls them? ***Hunks of metal.*** Look closely, and you will see that the slot for the fire control group isn't milled out.

Additionally, none of the holes for the trigger or hammer pins have been drilled. This is what's called an *80% lower* because it's only 80% done. 80% receivers are to date available for all sorts of weapons — pistols such as 1911s, as well as rifles such as AK, AR, and FAL variants among others. There's a thriving market in 80% lowers today, because people want to take advantage of the many benefits an 80% receiver provides:

- Exempt from background checks, fees, or forms
- Can finish it off yourself
- Can be bought over the counter at will
- Totally anonymous and untraceable

Finishing off an 80% receiver to make it a 100% receiver is a task that varies in difficulty depending on what style receiver you are building; most 80% manufacturers also supply jigs and detailed plans for finishing the receiver off. Usually, the finish work on an 80% receiver can be done with some common hand tools and a drill press. Of course, one set of jigs can be used for countless 80% receivers, so they just about pay for themselves. When you're finished with an 80% receiver, you basically wind up with a 100% receiver, or a full on firearm. This part now becomes a controlled part just like any other store bought receiver. If you decide you want to sell it, you must properly mark the receiver with caliber and place of origin just like a store bought receiver has.

All said, a person could own a handful of 1911 pistols, an AK, a couple ARs, and an FAL without ever having made a purchase at a gun store save for parts, and without ever undergoing a background check or filling out a 4473. 80% receivers are a little bit of freedom that you can buy *today*, and finish with simple hand tools at home.

Additionally, if you are worried about registration schemes or people coming after the guns you already own, you could simply buy 80% receivers, finish them, and substitute them for the ones on your current guns. You could always surrender the receivers that came with your firearm, or destroy them.

# KNOW YOUR LAWS

Keep in mind that many of the laws on America's books are quite old, dating back to the founding of the Republic. Property laws and firearms laws are two examples of fundamental laws that are fairly old, mainly because the concepts within these laws derive from the Constitution itself. Deep State can't easily defeat these laws because they can't easily erase the influence of the Constitution, so they try to pass new laws and regulations that are an attempt to weaken existing laws.

Firearms ownership has always been a prime target of the Deep State. For example, the 2nd Amendment to the US Constitution clearly defines firearms ownership as virtually unlimited. All kinds of laws have been passed that have infringed and watered down this amendment, and on top of that, ATF regulations have bound it further. Nowhere in the Constitution does it state that a shotgun with a barrel length less than 18" is illegal; the National Firearms Act of 1934 made it so.

What this means to you, Joe Citizen, enemy of the Deep State, is that you must know your laws inside and out, because many of them cannot easily be changed by the Deep State and they are considered to be "loopholes". Loophole is a term invented by the Deep State to villainize things that are perfectly legal. As an example, purchasing a firearm from another individual without a background check and without the services of a gun dealer is legal in many of the 50 states. Deep State calls such a purchase a "loophole" to make it sound like its wrong.

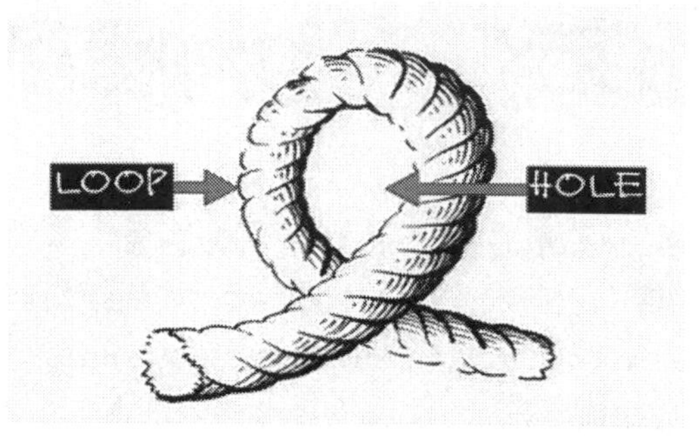


Actively search for these loopholes, and you will find the things that are 100% legal but the Deep State doesn't want you to know about. The onus is on you, the American Citizen, to know what your rights are. Don't take this burden lightly; study and learn the laws of the country within which you live.

# IF YOU CAN'T BEAT THEM, JOIN THEM

Deep State can only be countered by good Americans willing to fight them, and sometimes that means fighting them at their own game. Becoming a part of government, the military, or even the police is much easier than you think. America is unique in that it allows working individuals to take side gigs (for lack of a better term) in very important missions. Here are some examples:

- **Reserve Police Officer:** Worried about what the police will do in times of crisis? Find out by becoming one. A police reserve often works one or two days per month, usually without pay, but still has the authority and most importantly, the training and equipment of a full time officer. There is no better way to fight the militarization and heavy handedness of the police than to become one, and change the department from within. Police reserves have access to high tech weapons and training that's not available to civilians.
- **CERT or Search and Rescue member:** CERT stands for Community Emergency Response Team, and almost every city has a program to take normal citizens and turn them into search and rescue operatives for when the crap hits the fan. By becoming a CERT team member, or even volunteer firefighter, you will get specialized training for emergencies and be included in your city's emergency plan. This gives you a really clear picture as to what the authorities are planning to do during an emergency.

- **Military Reservist:** By joining your state's National or State Guard, you can put in a couple of days per month and learn how to use the highest tech weapons on the planet, plus, you will get the inside scoop on what your state's military plans are during emergencies. Many people are afraid of the military; by joining a Guard or Reserve MP (military police) unit, you will ensure that you have access to all of the contingency plans for your area. 
- **City Council or City Hall Volunteer:** There are a surprising amount of openings for volunteer positions within your local city hall, most of which are underfunded and desperately need people. City hall is a great place to hear what's happening in your area, and many Deep State plans are pushed down to City Hall from county and state governments.

The theme here is beating Deep State at its own game by embedding yourself within the apparatus and learning and avoiding their evil plans. Half the battle is knowing what they are going to do, and by getting closer to them, you will hear many, many things that the public is not privy to.

# CONCLUSION

The biggest threat facing the nation today is not North Korea, it's not Russia — it's not any outside force. Know that Deep State concocts many of these boogeymen to suit its purposes, always keeping the American people afraid of some external threat when the real threat is within. Your goal is to stay as anonymous as possible, and be ready for whatever comes up. Most likely, when the Deep State reveals its hand of cards, it will do so in the form of some local disaster on American soil, where it can seize power in the midst of crisis. Many of the preparations you'll want to make for such an event mimic that of regular natural disasters. Stay ready!